Contents

C000181221

Superstitions – sense or nonsense?

Remember Macbeth, that monstrous ambitious Scottish bloke in the play by William Shakespeare? (No? Well go and read it then. Come on, chop chop!) Did you know that actors get very nervous if you call the play "Macbeth"? They say it brings bad luck. You have to call it "The Scottish Play". Yes, I know it seems ridiculous, but it's a superstition that actors have, even if they're really famous.

Are you superstitious? Do you always put the left leg into your trousers first and hop about to avoid the cracks between the floorboards? Have you ever asked yourself if it really is lucky to rip your trousers and fall flat on your face every morning? Thought not. It just doesn't make any sense to me!

Here are my top 12 superstitions (I was planning to have 13, but 13's an unlucky number, isn't it?) ...

1. It's bad luck to walk under a ladder.

Think about this one. Is it good luck to step out into the road to avoid walking under the ladder, getting your toes crushed by the Number 15 bus and spending three long weeks in hospital?

2. Having a black cat cross your path is very bad luck.

What if you actually own a black cat? Does it mean your life will be one long disaster unless you play a continuous game of hide and seek, or lock yourself in the bedroom 24/7?

3. Breaking a mirror brings seven years' bad luck.

They say it's because a mirror is a reflection of your soul. I say it's because your dad refuses to give you even a penny of pocket money until you've paid for a new mirror. Tight or what?

4. Hanging a horseshoe over the door brings good luck.

But what if you don't bang the nails in properly and it falls on your head?

Oh goody! I'm in casualty with an enormous lump the size of three boiled eggs on my head. Yippee!

5. On the subject of boiled eggs, when you finish eating one they say: **it's good luck to push your spoon through the bottom of the egg.**

Then out come the last runny bits you didn't eat ... all over your trousers. Marvellous.

6. It's bad luck to put your left shoe on your right foot.

How can that be? Hmm, let's think ... you look ridiculous, your mates make fun of you and you fall over.

7. It's bad luck to put a shirt on inside-out.

Same as 6 – you look ridiculous, only without the falling over bit.

8. If a baby doesn't sneeze before it's 12 months old, it will grow up to be a fool.

If you're curious, all you have to do is watch a baby – they sneeze all the time! If a baby doesn't sneeze before it's 12 months old, it's not a baby, it's a plastic doll!

9. It's bad luck to pass somebody on the stairs.

How am I supposed to get upstairs?
Who do you think I am? Harry Potter?

10. If you put your toenail clippings in a glass of lemonade, the person who drinks it will fall in love with you.

Fabulous! Would you want to spend your life with a person who sticks toenails in your drinks? Well, would you? Warning: don't try this one at the weekend because it's bad luck to cut your nails on a Friday or Saturday ... so they say.

11. I love this one:

It's bad luck to mend clothes while you're actually wearing them.

Well, obviously!

Oh dear – the zip on my trousers has just gone, but I won't bother taking them off, I'll just poke about with this ferociously sharp needle!

12. It's good luck if a bird poos on your head.

Are you serious??

A famous writer – *Shakespeare*

The whining schoolboy, with his satchel
And shining morning face, creeping like snail
Unwillingly to school.

Do you know who wrote these humorous lines? They were written more than 400 years ago, in a play called *As You Like It*. The writer? William Shakespeare. Are you curious about this man? Want to know more?

1564 William was born in Stratford-upon-Avon. His parents were Mary Arden and John Shakespeare. He had seven brothers and sisters, but three of them died when they were children.

John Shakespeare was a glove maker and wool merchant, but it's likely that he did not know how to read or write. We think that his ambitious son, William, went to King's New School in Stratford, where he learned these skills.

In Shakespeare's time, there were more than 80 different ways of spelling his name.

Birth Certificate

~~Shakespere~~
~~Shackspeare~~
~~Shaxpere~~
Shakespeare

Nobody knows Shakespeare's true birthday!

1582 William married Anne Hathaway, a farmer's daughter. He was 18 and she was 26.

1583 William and Anne had a baby girl, Susanna.

1585 Twins, Hamnet and Judith, were born.

An adventurous young man, William went to London to write plays and poems. London was a dangerous place, with many of its inhabitants suffering from serious diseases.

1593 A plague broke out in London and all the plays were cancelled.

1596 William's precious son Hamnet died, aged 11.

After these events, William wrote some of his darkest plays, like *Macbeth*, full of hideous happenings and murderous characters.

There are no relatives of Shakespeare living today – the last of his grandchildren died in the 1600s.

Actors say that it is bad luck to call the play *Macbeth* by its name. They call it "The Scottish Play".

1599 The Globe Theatre opened in London, showing William's plays.

The Globe Theatre was destroyed by fire in 1613, but an updated Globe Theatre still shows Shakespeare's plays today. An episode of *Doctor Who*, starring David Tennant, was filmed there.

After writing numerous plays, William returned to Stratford.

1616 William Shakespeare died.

Shakespeare died on his 52nd birthday (or at least it is thought he did!)

In his will, Shakespeare left his 'second-best' bed to his wife, Anne. (His best bed was for guests.)

In his plays, Shakespeare used a lot of insults.
Let's hope that no one ever says any of these to you!

You are ...

a loathsome scab

a man of wax

a tedious fool

a slug

a most villainous knave

a jealous, rascally knave

a poisonous,
hunch-backed toad

a starved snake

a puke-stocking

a ravenous fish

foul and dangerous

like the toad,
ugly and venomous

We still use some of Shakespeare's phrases today. *Do you know these?*

Phrase	Meaning
a dish fit for the gods	a delicious dish
eaten out of house and home	eaten all my food
the green-eyed monster	jealousy
fight fire with fire	fight in the same way as your attacker
all that glitters is not gold	a pretty thing is not always valuable
a fool's paradise	happiness based on false hope

You may say, why didn't Shakespeare write in plain English? Well, he did! But in those times, English was very different. Also, there were fewer words and no dictionaries, and writers simply made up their own words when they wanted to.

Sounds like a fun way to write plays!

A terrible day in Pompeii

On 23rd August in AD79, people in the city of Pompeii were celebrating Vulcan, the Roman god of fire. They thought he worked at his furnace under ground in the nearby volcano, Mount Vesuvius. They went to bed as usual that night, but they didn't know that the next day, many of them would die. And the survivors would think that their underground god Vulcan was responsible!

Pompeii

Two thousand years ago, Pompeii was a large, busy city in the south of Italy. It was a port, a place of business, and a holiday resort. There were plenty of shops, theatres and temples, and a bustling market place. Rich Romans had large houses there, with pretty gardens.

But Pompeii was only 8km from Mount Vesuvius. Volcanoes are unpredictable, and no one knew how much at risk their city was.

The volcano erupts

On 24th August, everybody went about their business as usual. There had been some slight earth tremors during the night, but nothing remarkable.

If you had a donkey, or a dog, you might have noticed that the animal was restless for some reason. And there were a few white clouds in the sky – no one knew they were really clouds of volcanic gas.

At about 1 p.m. the unthinkable happened. Mount Vesuvius erupted. Disaster was unavoidable as a huge cloud of red-hot gas, ash and rock blew out. Unstoppable, and moving at a speed of 720 km per hour, it completely covered the city of Pompeii. Everyone panicked, and large numbers fled. Some tried to escape by sea, but many people and animals suffocated or burned to death. Pompeii was now almost invisible – only the tops of tall buildings could be seen.

Afterwards

After the terrible disaster, rescue parties were organised by the survivors.
But it was an impossible task, and they managed to rescue only a few statues
and other valuables. Thousands of people were homeless and penniless,
and unbearably miserable. The belongings of those who had died were sold to
raise money.

There were plans to dig out the city and live in it again. But understandably,
it was a hopeless task. In time, trees and grass grew over the site, and new
buildings were put up. The Roman city of Pompeii was forgotten.

Uncovering the invisible city

Fifteen hundred years later, in 1594,
workmen were digging out a water
channel on the site. They found some
walls with paintings on them. But no
one took much notice. In those days,
people weren't interested in digging
up the past.

In 1689, more workmen found a stone with the word 'POMPEIA' carved on it.
Then, in 1706, more painted walls were found, and so tunnels were dug.
Many Roman treasures were removed.

In 1748, the Roman city of Pompeii was recognisable after serious digging.
In the 1800s, the King of Italy organised a dig, making proper plans and records.
Detailed plaster models were made of some of the victims.

Pompeii today

Digging continues today. Pompeii is no longer invisible. It's possible to visit the site, where you will be able to go in and out of the buildings and gardens, and see the remains of:

- grand houses
- the forum (market place)
- the amphitheatre where gladiators and animals probably fought
- shopping streets
- a laundry
- a bar
- a bakery and a millstone
- bronze statues
- paintings and mosaics
- a sports ground with a swimming pool

You can also see some Roman graffiti! People dislike graffiti today, but these wall scribblings tell us a lot about the Romans and their daily lives. And if you're feeling incredibly brave, it's possible to climb to the top of Mount Vesuvius, and even see into the crater!

Mission impossible!

5th August 2010

Terrible news has just come in from San Jose copper mine in Chile. An unstable roof has collapsed, leaving 33 miners trapped deep underground, unreachable.

The first rumblings above their heads told the miners that something was seriously wrong. They immediately fled to the emergency room, or refuge. There, nearly 700 metres below ground, foreman Luis Urzua began to organise his men.

When the dust cleared, a group was sent out of the refuge to explore. What they found chilled their blood – huge rocks had left their escape route impassable. Next they tried the narrow, vertical ventilation shafts, but missing ladders made them unclimbable. They were trapped!

All they could do now was try to stay alive ... and hope. Food was sensibly rationed, and drinkable water was taken from the radiators of stranded trucks. They used the trucks' batteries to power their head torches.

The heat was unbearable, and the men were faced with the challenge of staying healthy. One miner was made responsible for medicines. Although he wasn't a doctor, he had to treat injuries and illnesses. Their future unpredictable, they battled to keep each other's spirits up while they waited to be rescued.

Every two days each miner had to survive on:

- two spoonfuls of tuna
- one sip of milk
- half a cracker

Above ground, families watched and waited. They set up tents to live in, and local villagers brought them food. This new temporary home was named Camp Hope. Skilled engineers drilled narrow holes in the ground to try to locate the refuge, but as maps of the mine were unreliable, it was an almost impossible task. Then, on Day 17, a huge cheer echoed around the valley. Unbelievably, a drill had come back up to the surface with a note attached:

We are all well in the refuge.

The 33.

Supplies could now be sent down – bottled water, food and medicine, followed by a video camera. At long last the stranded miners were visible to the rest of the world. But could they be saved? And if so, how long would it take?

Scientists told the miners to switch lights off between 9 p.m. and 8 a.m. to try to simulate day and night. This would enable their bodies to keep to a normal daily routine.

A tiny projector was sent down so that the miners were able to watch Chile take on Ukraine in a live football match. Unfortunately Chile lost 2–1.

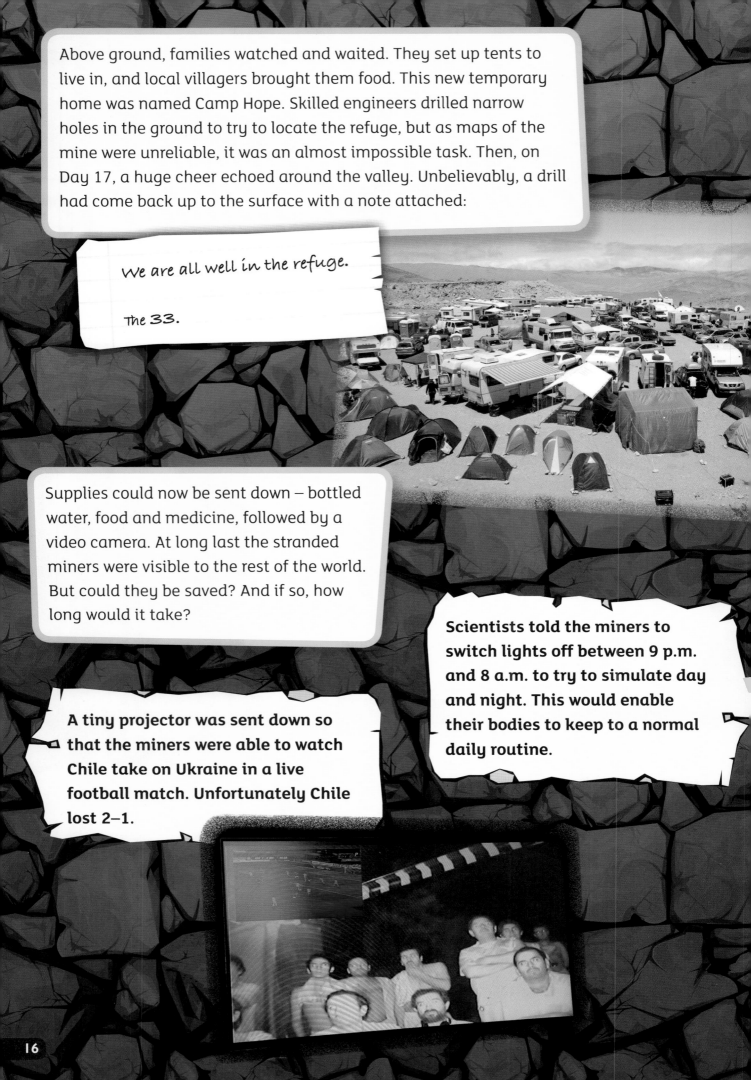

Now the engineers set about the considerable task of building a one-man escape capsule that could be lowered down to the miners. Space rocket experts gave advice, helping to create the life-saving device, named Fenix 2.

Twist-resistant cable

Helmet with built-in communication system

Wheels to guide capsule through shaft

Heart rate monitor

Eye protection

If Fenix 2 became trapped, a release catch would allow it to be lowered back down again.

Safety harness

Oxygen supply

The miners had to shift the tons of rubble that fell as the drill hole was widened to allow Fenix 2 to pass. Finally it arrived, and one by one they began the 15–20 minute journey to freedom, squeezed uncomfortably into the capsule.

Each arrival at the surface was greeted with cheers as well as tears of joy. Luis Urzua was the last to leave the refuge. On 13th October 2010, 69 days after disaster had struck, wearing sunglasses to protect his eyes, he stepped out of Fenix 2 to a hero's welcome. The most incredible rescue operation in history was complete.

Mission accomplished!

So what happened next?

Surviving over two months trapped underground earned the miners a place in the *Guinness Book of Records*.

Miner Edison Pena had kept himself fit by running nearly 10 kilometres a day through the tunnels. Just 25 days after his dramatic rescue, he took part in the New York Marathon. Still wearing dark glasses, and with ice strapped to his injured knee, he completed the course in 5 hours, 40 minutes.

Two months after being rescued, 23 of the miners were guests of honour at the football match between Manchester United and Arsenal. They were photographed with Manchester United legend, Sir Bobby Charlton, whose father had been a miner.

The miners now

Since the rescue, some of the miners have had health problems. Believe it or not, others have carried on mining! A film called "The 33" came out in 2015 which retold their story.

Ballad of a pirate of distinction!

Whitebeard was a pirate,
But a gentle soul was he.
While his pirate pals were plotting,
He was sipping a nice cup of tea.

They'd all meet up in the tavern,
For story-swapping sessions.
Their tales were tough,
Their talk was rough –
Where was Whitebeard? Elocution lessons!

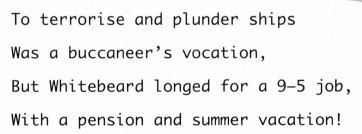

To terrorise and plunder ships
Was a buccaneer's vocation,
But Whitebeard longed for a 9–5 job,
With a pension and summer vacation!

Captain Sam had a cutlass, sharp,
Mad Jack had a wicked eye,
Bad Harry had a hook
and a very nasty look,
But Whitebeard? He wouldn't hurt a fly.

Once at sea, conditions were bad –
Pirate ships had a certain, er, stink.
Bodies and clothes were rarely washed,
But Whitebeard was a vision – in pink!

You might well ask why Whitebeard,
Had chosen this harsh occupation?
Well, press-ganged into the Navy,
He then fled, in desperation.

He fled with the pirates who'd raided his ship.
Their mission had been to destroy
The splendid vessel and capture her crew,
But Whitebeard was just a boy.

Captain Sam was the pirate in charge
Of that fateful operation –
To board the good ship 'Invincible',
And imprison the population.

In the bloody battle that then took place,
There was fighting without hesitation.
Captain Sam and his ruthless gang
Lived up to their fierce reputation.

As they raided the ship for its riches,
Silver and golden bars,
Captain Sam spotted a cabin boy
Hiding behind some jars.

Hard as he was, Sam was softened
By the poor lad's situation.
Instead of taking him prisoner, he thought,
"I'll give him an education!"

He named him after his father,
Raised him like his own flesh and blood,
But Whitebeard hated the pirate life,
He just wanted to be, well, good.

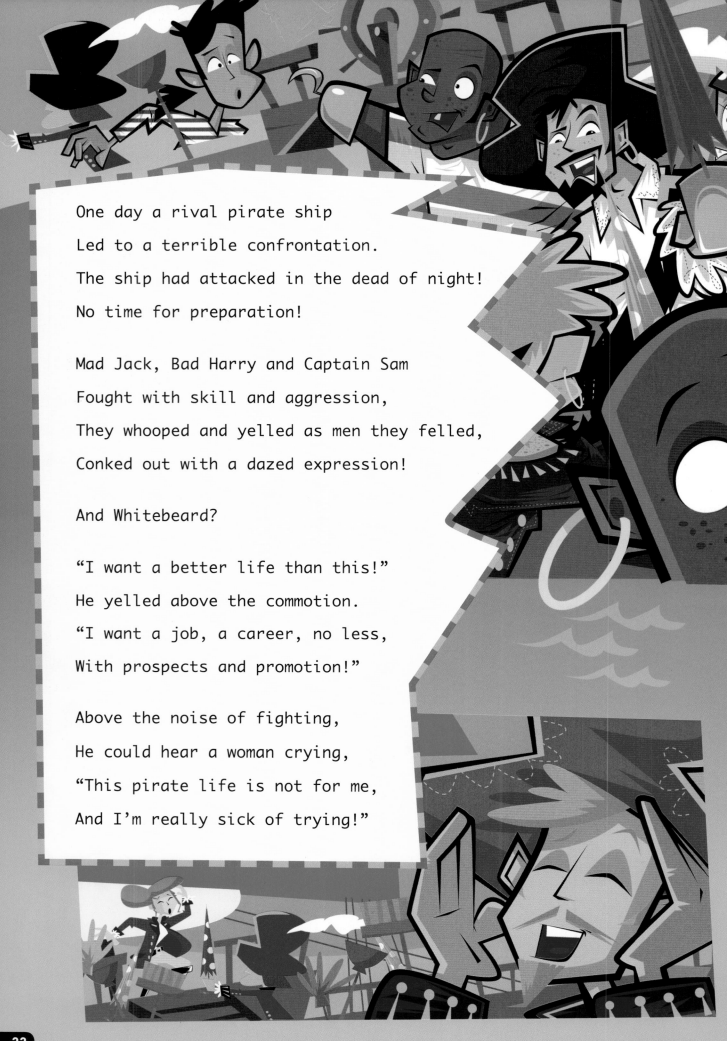

One day a rival pirate ship
Led to a terrible confrontation.
The ship had attacked in the dead of night!
No time for preparation!

Mad Jack, Bad Harry and Captain Sam
Fought with skill and aggression,
They whooped and yelled as men they felled,
Conked out with a dazed expression!

And Whitebeard?

"I want a better life than this!"
He yelled above the commotion.
"I want a job, a career, no less,
With prospects and promotion!"

Above the noise of fighting,
He could hear a woman crying,
"This pirate life is not for me,
And I'm really sick of trying!"

Suddenly, they were face to face —
A truly momentous occasion.
They were meant to fight to the end of course,
But they started a conversation!

Jolly Jen was a pirate girl,
Dressed in the latest fashion.
When she spotted Whitebeard's pink, silk suit,
She fell in love - clothes were her passion.

Hand in hand they walked the plank
(They both made quick decisions).
They swam to the nearest country,
That they knew would have provisions.

They married and started a business
Selling clothes in their perfect location.
At last, Whitebeard and Jolly Jen
Had found their true vocation!

Pirate application pack

The pirate ship *Fresh Blood* is in the process of recruiting a new crew.

Interested?

Then please read this helpful information before sending in your application.

Qualifications

You must be young, fit, strong, not afraid to break the law and willing to fight. Education is not necessary, and a criminal record may actually help your application! All applicants must be male.

Pirates had many superstitions – one of which was that females brought bad luck on board a ship.

Job description

During periods of calm, you will be required to:

⚓ patch up sails damaged by cannonball fire

⚓ make and mend ropes

⚓ seal any cracks between planks with hot tar to keep the ship watertight

⚓ keep your weapons clean and ready to use.

Bored pirates would get irritable, and then trouble would often start. In their spare time, pirates would sing, dance or carve wooden ornaments. They would also play cards and dice, but gambling was banned as it caused fights.

When fighting against another ship, you will be expected to:
- ⚓ obey instructions from the captain, without exception
- ⚓ fight to the death.

Your rights

As a valued crew member, you will have a vote in the election of the captain, and also in any decision on whether or not to attack an enemy ship. You will receive your fair share of gold, silver or any other treasure following a successful raid.

Piracy was hardly a steady job. Pirates didn't know if their next trip might be their last. Once ashore in a friendly port, it was quite common for pirates to spend all their share of the treasure in a single night, on luxuries such as fine food and drink.

Regulations

- ⚓ You shall not attempt to run away in the heat of battle.
- ⚓ You shall not strike another crew member.
- ⚓ You shall not steal from another crew member.

In the event of such regulations not being obeyed, you will be put in front of a court consisting of your fellow crew members. If found guilty, the following punishments may be applied:

⚓ confiscation of shares in treasure

⚓ marooning on a desert island with just one bottle of water and a small supply of food

⚓ walking the plank.

Provisions
Information on diet will be provided once the applicant is at sea.

It's not surprising they didn't want to go into details about food. A pirate's diet was, for the most part, disgusting. Although fresh fish could be caught on occasion, most meals consisted of mouldy meat and hard tack. This was a tough, dry biscuit – very likely infested by weevils and nibbled by rats. Water was stale and virtually undrinkable.

Dress regulations

A shirt, waistcoat and three-quarter length trousers are the usual uniform, with bare feet. Waistcoats may be coated with tar as added protection against swords.

Accommodation

'Compact' and 'cosy' are descriptions that have been supplied by previous successful applicants.

Compact and cosy? Well, I suppose that's one way of putting it. Pirates' living conditions were disgraceful. Crammed in like sardines, they never washed, so the place would be a dark, stinking pit. Rats would roam freely, and any disease spread quickly.

Health care

Due to the nature of the job, the management cannot accept any responsibility for death in the line of duty. However, compensation will be awarded for loss of limbs.

Five-star medical care? Forget it! Pirate crews would not include a doctor, so operations would usually be carried out by the ship's carpenter or cook! 'Pass the bread knife, Jim, me old mate!'

Applications can be made in person to Captain Jack Treasure at Ye Olde Shippe Inn, Plymouth harbour.

Grand theft
at Bagshot Manor

A serious robbery has taken place at Bagshot Manor, home of the fabulously rich Sir Clive Bubbly-Snap. Inspector Spratt has been called in to lead the investigation.

SUSPECT 1
HANK STOCK

◆ International strong man. He lifted a shop.

Sir Clive: So what do you think, Inspector Spratt?

Spratt: The front door appears to have been battered down, Sir Clive. No messing about with the lock, just plain brute force. It would take a man of enormous power to do a thing like that.

Sir Clive: You mean ... Hank Stock?

Spratt: Stock's dead, Sir Clive. It would be difficult to commit a robbery from underneath Rick's Gift Shop in Dallas. Let's stick to the living suspects, shall we?

Sir Clive: Who then?

Spratt: Well, from the traces of powder, it looks like the safe door's been torn off with explosives. Not a big charge – just enough to bring the door off without destroying the contents. What was in the safe, Sir Clive?

Sir Clive: £50,000 in cash, plus gold and silver jewels … and my valuable collection of DVDs. All gone.

Spratt: DVDs, did you say?

Sir Clive: That's right. About 300, various classic films.

Spratt: That could be the clue we're looking for, Sir Clive.

SUSPECT 2
Big Malc

◆ Caught shoplifting DVDs and choccy eggs last year.

Big Malc: Is this some sort of joke, Spratt? Cos if it is, it isn't funny!

Spratt: No joke, pal. I want information and I want it fast.

Big Malc: You're asking the wrong man, Inspector.

Spratt: The cash and the jewels, Big Malc. What have you done with them?

Big Malc: I've told you!

Spratt: Tell me again.

Big Malc: I haven't got them, and I've never had them. Until you dragged me here tonight, I'd never set foot in this place. Jewels and money aren't my game.

Spratt: But DVDs are, Big Malc, and grand theft can easily follow if a man's desperate enough.

Big Malc: Look, Spratt – I may be a crook, but how am I supposed to pull a stunt like this? How could these weedy arms batter down a door that size? It's impossible! Plus the fact that I only got back from flogging my latest batch of dodgy DVDs in Manchester today. Oops! What I mean is, I only just returned from a successful sales trip to the north of England.

Spratt: I know what you mean, Big Malc. I'm not a complete idiot.

Big Malc: Really, Inspector? You could have fooled me. Look you can't pin this job on me, and you know it. If I were you, I'd start with those strands of hay covering the carpet. Bit odd, don't you think?

SUSPECT 3
Rumpelstiltskin

♦ Spins hay into gold. Well-known for his nasty tricks.

Rumpelstiltskin: This is ridiculous!
If I had a lawyer, I'd demand to see him. What's this all about, Spratt?

Spratt: Grand theft, that's what this is about. And hay.

Rumpelstiltskin: Hay? So look for a horse!

Spratt: Horses are bright, but not that bright. No, the hay points to only one man. Devious, cunning … and nasty. Just about sums you up, doesn't it, Rumpelstiltskin?

Rumpelstiltskin: Devious I may be, but I'm no thief, Spratt.

Spratt: Maybe not in the past, Rumps, but you could change. You're the sort who would stop at nothing to get what you want. And you're mighty strong for a small man.

Rumpelstiltskin: Granted, Spratt. But you're missing one important point.

Spratt: And what's that?

Rumpelstiltskin: Explosives don't exist in my world. I'm fiction. Fairy-tale fiction. Strictly no explosives. I'm not your man, Spratt, but I reckon I know who is.

Spratt: Go on then – spill the beans, Shorty.

Rumpelstiltskin: No need to get personal, Spratt. If you had my nose, you'd have the robber behind bars by now.

Spratt: What are you rattling on about, Stilts?

Rumpelstiltskin: That smell, Spratt. I'd recognise it anywhere … beef sandwich.

SUSPECT 4
Norman Knight

◆ Time-travelling footballer.

Spratt: Now then Norman …

Norman Knight: Mr Knight, if you please, Inspector.

Spratt: Very well … Mr Knight. Where exactly were you on the night of 5th May?

Norman Knight: Is that 5th May 2017, 1987, 1947 or 1907, Inspector?

Spratt: Cut the nonsense, Knight – I haven't got the time.

Norman Knight: *You* may not, Inspector, but I have. I'm a time-travelling superstar, remember? On 5th May 1907, for example, I was playing in the FA Cup Final for Stockpot County. In 2017, on the other hand, I was at an after-match dinner following Ashton Villa's Cup victory over Chillsea Chuggers.

Spratt: The theft took place after midnight, Knight. You had plenty of time to get here from London. You're strong, too. Strong enough to hammer down a door, maybe. I hear you're still on 1907 wages. Five shillings a week doesn't go very far these days. £50,000 though, that's a different story. And then there's the sandwich – you can't resist a good beef sandwich, so I'm told.

Norman Knight: When you put it like that, it sounds so believable, Inspector. But you're overlooking one thing.

Spratt: Go on – surprise me.

Norman Knight: I'd just eaten a ten-course dinner at the Ritz Hotel, including twelve portions of roast beef. I may be a big eater, but I have my limits. Are you seriously saying that I left the Ritz, sped down here from London, robbed the safe, then made myself comfortable with a nice home-made beef sandwich? When my belly was already fit to burst? Incredible! You're looking in the wrong direction, Inspector. Maybe that shred of torn tartan fabric under the table could be the clue you're after.

SUSPECT 5
Macbeth

◆ Ambitious and ruthless Scottish nobleman.

Macbeth: Theft!? Who is it that dares to stand before me and question me about theft? A brave and strong man, I trust, or he'll see the mighty swing of my axe!

Spratt: Easy, easy, Mr Macbeth — no need to lose your cool. I must tell you that I have fifteen armed men outside in case of problems.

Macbeth: Fifteen? Ha! Do not insult the true King of Scotland, you feeble English pup!

Spratt: Can we get back to the theft please, Mr Macbeth? I take it you deny stealing the money and jewels?

Macbeth: Aye, that I do. Have ye no eyes in that head of yours? Have ye not seen the footprints that lie outside the window? They're footprints of a giant, a man I'd be proud to have in my army, to march alongside into battle. A true monster of a man!

Spratt: Hmm. A monster of a man, you say? Or maybe just ... a monster. I think I've got it!

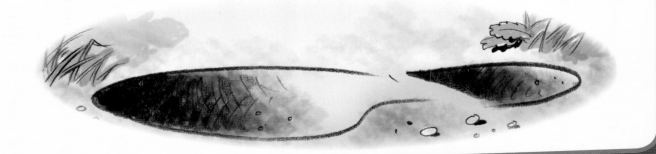

SUSPECT 6

Frankenstein's Monster

Boggins: We've sent out a description to police units up and down the country, and set up checkpoints on all roads, airports and seaports, sir. He won't get far. Not a man his size, he's too obvious. We'll soon have the thief behind bars.

Spratt: Thank you, Boggins. You can go now.

Sir Clive: Size, Spratt?

Spratt: Yes, Sir Clive. It hit me as soon as Macbeth mentioned the footprint. There's only one man that could leave that print and batter down that front door. Frankenstein's monster. But I don't think he worked alone on this job. He had the power, but not the brains.

Sir Clive: What do you mean?

Spratt: The monster was here, but not to steal the jewels. He and the real thief hid in the barn until the coast was clear, that's the reason for the hay on the floor. The monster smashed down the door, and then he was probably paid off and he left. The thief then entered the house and stole the contents of the safe. But there was one problem. She realised there was a witness.

Sir Clive: She? You think this was a woman's work?

Spratt: I'm sure of it, Sir Clive. Did you spot the empty hamster cage? Kevin the hamster was the witness!

Sir Clive: Kevin! Nooooooo!

Spratt: It looks like he put up a real fight, biting and scratching, even ripping a scrap of tartan from the thief's jacket, but in the end he had no chance. She took him away with her.

Sir Clive: Aaaaagggghhhhh! Poor Kevin!

Spratt: Pull yourself together, Sir Clive. If we take the next train, we should arrive in London before Amy Oliver's TV show begins. We'll rescue Kevin and we'll get her to cook us dinner. A tasty hot meal ... from a vicious, cold thief!

Survivors

Palm leaves drooped lazily in the warm air. Rippling waves lapped at the golden sand. Distant squawks signalled that the jungle was waking up to a new day. The first rays of sun peeped over the hills, gradually revealing the motionless figures that lay there beneath the trees.

One of the shapes stirred. It sat up. It opened its mouth. "Look at the state of my hair! Just *look* at it! **And where's my breakfast?!**"

If anyone heard, they didn't show it. They'd already put up with two full days of non-stop moaning. Shutting their ears to the whining voice, they rolled over and went back to sleep.

Snow White would have to wait for her breakfast.

"Why did the publishers arrange the party for Fresh Start characters in Japan, anyway?" grumbled grumpy Shakespeare. "I mean what's wrong with London, or Stratford-upon-Avon? Somewhere that didn't involve plane travel."

"Or plane crashes," added Snow White bitterly.

"Nice place, Japan," mumbled Thog shyly. "And not that far away really."

"Maybe not for an alien from the Black Planet, who's travelled about 55 zillion light years just to get in on a free party!" snarled Snow White. "Besides, you might have noticed that we're not actually in Japan!"

Thog shrank back into the shadows. He'd always been bashful with females.

"I can't understand how the pilot and crew could use all the parachutes and leave us to fend for ourselves," groaned Shakespeare.

"Oh don't be so grumpy, Shakes mate," grinned Louis Squelch. "Just look at the good points. In no particular order: the trees cushioned our landing, we all survived, and now we're through to boot camp in paradise!"

"Paradise, you idiot?" snapped Snow White. "It's a jungle out there."

"That's show business, Snowy, old girl. Get used to it!"

"This is **not** show business, Louis. It's reality TV … without the cameras. There are all kinds of horrible deadly creatures just waiting for a chance to get their teeth into us!"

"Excellent!" Wild Mike rubbed his hands together in anticipation. "Bring it on!"

It was a strange group of misfits that sat on the sand to eat their meal together – trays of cold chicken pasta taken from the wrecked aircraft. Between Shakespeare and Thog sat the Cyclops, his one huge eye blinking and bloodshot from lack of sleep. Amy Oliver pursed her lips in disgust. This was certainly not the quality of food she was used to – what would her TV followers think? To her left, Cake-face Jake's head dropped on to Wild Mike's shoulder, and he began to snore quietly.

"Shouldn't we send some kind of signal?" suggested Amy, when breakfast was done. "I mean they must be searching for us, surely?" She sneezed daintily into her hanky. "Drat! I wish I could get rid of this hay fever!"

"I could've called them on my mobile, if that dopey Cyclops hadn't trodden on it and crushed it!" cursed Snow White.

"It's alright for you to moan," blinked the Cyclops. "When *you* get sand in your eye, you've got another one to see out of."

"Stop snivelling!" snapped Snow White. "Wild Mike will sort your eye out. He's supposed to be good with jungle medicines."

"Oh, cheer up, you two," chuckled Louis. "Amy's right. Maybe we should write a message in the sand for any passing aircraft to see."

"As the greatest writer in the history of the English language," said Shakespeare, "I feel that I should take care of that task. Want to help, Jake?"

But the only reply was a quiet snore.

"Right – let's get organised." Snow White was back where she belonged – in control. "Cyclops, now that Wild Mike's sorted your eye problem out, you'll be our guard. It's your job to keep your eye out for wild animals. Thog, you'll go into the jungle with Wild Mike to find us some food. As for you, Jake, now you've finally woken up, you can stay here and keep the camp clean and tidy."

Jake wasn't impressed. "I don't mean to be rude, but … er … isn't that *your* job? I mean, in all the films you've always got a broom in your hand, sweeping up. And I'm too tired to tidy up."

Snow White fixed Jake with a withering glare. "Who's in charge here, Jake?" she hissed.

Jake gulped and cowered away from her. "Y-you are, Snowy."

"Good. I'm glad we had that little chat. Now get lost and start raiding the plane for pillows, cooking gear and anything else that looks as if it'll come in handy."

"What about me?" asked Amy Oliver meekly, when Jake had fled.

"You're no use to anyone while you're sneezing your head off like that. Maybe Wild Mike can find some kind of plant or herb in the jungle that'll cure it. In the meantime, just stay out of my way."

The day wore on. Eventually, in the late evening, trampling sounds were heard. Mike and Thog emerged from the jungle, carrying a wild deer and a bag full of mouth-watering fruits.

"Grub's up!" whooped Mike. "Amy, get cooking!"

"Good idea," said Snow White. "Wake Jake up. He can cut the fruit."

"That's odd," wondered Amy out loud. "Where *is* Jake? I haven't seen him since you sent him back to the plane."

They searched the camp. They searched the beach. They searched the trees nearby. There was no sign of Jake. He'd disappeared into the jungle.

The evening meal was not a success. While Wild Mike acted as doc and treated Amy's hay fever, Thog took over cooking duties.

"What on earth is this supposed to be?" wailed Snow White, a forkful of crispy blackened meat in her hand.

"Sorry," mumbled Thog shyly.

"Black planet, black food. I suppose it fits," she added cruelly.

Louis came to the rescue. "Don't be too harsh on poor bashful Thog. He gave 110 per cent. As our mentor, you clearly chose the wrong chef."

"We're going to starve," moaned Shakespeare. "And it's all **your** fault."

"Me?! **You've** no room to talk, Mister Grumpy!" snapped Snow White. "Great job you made of that message in the sand!"

"It was poetic."

"It was rubbish! By the time any pilot finished reading it, they'd have fallen asleep at the controls. How did it start? Let's remember, shall we?

'To ye who soars, bird-like amongst the clouds,

If ye should lower thy shining eyes

And gaze down from thy lofty perch,

Thou mayst just see, marooned below …'

What's wrong with a simple '**Help!!!**' for goodness' sake?"

The reply wasn't heard. The greatest author in history had already stomped off into the jungle, never to return.

At daybreak the following morning, Wild Mike and Thog took to the jungle on their second hunt for food. By mid-afternoon, there was still no sign of them.

"Do you think we should send out a search party?" suggested Amy nervously.

"Consisting of who?" snarled Snow White through gritted teeth. "A clumsy, one-eyed, dopey monster, a sneezy wimp of a TV chef, or a ridiculously happy, grinning judge?"

"Well I don't intend to sit here and do nothing. I'm off." Picking up her wooden spoon as a weapon, Amy stomped off towards the trees. "You coming, Cyclops?"

"Suppose so," muttered the miserable myth. "Someone's got to keep an eye on you."

And that was the last anyone saw of them.

Night fell. Buzzing insects circled, diving now and then to take a stinging bite.

Snow White broke the broody silence. "So, just the two of us left, eh, Louis? You scared?"

"Don't be silly!" he laughed. "Someone will save us. We're famous, remember? They can't just let us die. Soon we'll be back home, safe and happy … " His voice trailed off.

"What's the matter, Louis? Why are you staring at me like that?"

"Happy … I'll be *happy.* Aha! It all adds up now."

"What all adds up? What are you on about?"

"First it was *sleepy* little Jake, then *grumpy* old Shakespeare. Next to disappear were *bashful* Thog, and Wild Mike, the group's *doc.* Then *sneezy* Amy and the *dopey* Cyclops. You've driven them all away into the jungle. Now all that's left is *happy* old me." His voice rose. "Am I next on your list, Snow White? Is that your devious plan? Am I next to be voted off?"

Snow White backed away. She took one look at the mad gleam in the judge's eyes, then turned and ran for the trees.

A group of seven missing fictional characters has been found safe and well on a remote tropical island. The search continues for the eighth member of the party, a Miss S. White.

Superstitions – sense or nonsense? (_ous _ious _eous _cious _tious)

Green words: *Say the syllables. Say the word.*

mon|strous   rid|ic|u|lous   fab|u|lous   en|or|mous   marv|ell|ous
con|tin|u|ous   am|bi|ti ous   su|per|sti|ti ous   nerv|ous

Red words: love   watch   through   th ought   doesn't

Challenge words: superstition   reflection   soul   breaking   months   famous
floorboards   sh oe   casualty   warning   wearing   serious

Vocabulary check: **casualty** *a hospital department for emergencies*
ferociously *fierce and savage*   **superstition** *something you believe that is not based on evidence*

A famous writer – Shakespeare (_ous _ious _eous _cious _tious)

Green words: *Say the syllables. Say the word.*

hum|or|ous   am|bi|ti ous   ad|ven|tur|ous   dan|ger|ous   pre|ci ous
hid|e|ous   mur|der|ous   nu|mer|ous   vill|ain|ous   ven|om|ous   ted|i|ous
de|li|ci ous   poi|son|ous   jeal|ous|y

Red words: th ought   broth ers

Challenge words: you ng   serious   plague   th eatre   dictionar ies
parents   glove   learned   daughter   guests   eyed   curious

Vocabulary check: **inhabitants** *people who live in a place*   **knave** *a dishonest man*
loathsome *causing hatred, repulsive*   **rascally** *a cheeky person*

A terrible day in Pompeii (_able _ably _ible _ibly)

Green words: *Say the syllables. Say the word.*

un|pre|dict|a|ble   in|vis|i|ble   terr|i|ble   poss|i|ble   im|poss|i|ble
mis|er|a|ble   un|stopp|a|ble   re|mark|a|ble   re|cog|nis|a|ble   un|think|a|ble
un|a|void|a|ble   re|spons|i|ble

Red words: th ought   many   water

Challenge words: amphitheatre   Pompeii   graffiti   Vesuvius   business
afterwards   fought   pretty   busy   volcano   earth   nothing   moving
covered   buildings   serious

Vocabulary check: **graffiti** *words or drawings usually made outside on walls*
amphitheatre *an arena where Romans watched gladiator and animals fight*
erupted *explode or blow up*

Mission impossible! (_able _ably _ible _ibly)

Green words: *Say the syllables. Say the word.*

im|poss|i|ble   terr|i|ble   un|sta|ble   un|rea ch|a|ble   im|pass|a|ble
un|climb|a|ble   un|pre|dict|a|ble   un|rel|i|a|ble   en|a|ble
con|sid|er|a|ble   in|cred|i|ble   sens|i|bly   un|be|liev|a|bly

Red words: could   would   through   water   above

Challenge words: Jose   seriously   routine   brought   journey   wearing   earned
guests   honour   Chile   blood   unbearable   half   engineers   world   building
heart   eye   guide   hero   cour se

Vocabulary check: **refuge** *safe shelter*   **foreman** *supervisor who directs other workers*
rationed *divided up to stop supplies from running out*   **simulate** *pretend to be like something*

Ballad of a pirate of distinction! (_tion _sion _ssion)

Green words: *Say the syllables. Say the word.*

des|per|a|tion   occ|u|pa|tion   vi|sion   con|di|tion   pro|mo|tion   dis|tinc|tion   el|o|cu|tion   vo|ca|tion   mi|ssion   pop|u|la|tion   hes|i|ta|tion   rep|u|ta|tion   con|fron|ta|tion   sit|u|a|tion   ed|u|ca|tion   pre|par|a|tion   agg|re|ssion   lo|ca|tion

Red words: th ought   talk   wouldn't   walked

Challenge words: fier ce   soul   washed   eye   board   fought   suit   cour se   tou gh   rou gh   business   swapping   blood   woman   country

Vocabulary check: **elocution lessons** *learning to speak in a "posh" voice*

distinction *showing excellence or individuality in a particular way*

vocation *something you are born to do*   **press-ganged** *forced or tricked into joining the Navy*

cutlass *kind of short sword with a curved blade*

Pirate application pack (_tion _sion _ssion)

Green words: *Say the syllables. Say the word.*

app|li|ca|tion   qual|i|fi|ca|tions   su|per|sti|tions   des|crip|tion   in|struc|tions   ex|cep|tion   el|ec|tion   reg|u|la|tions   con|fis|ca|tion   pro|vi|sions   o|cca|sion   pro|tec|tion   a|ccomm|o|da|tion   con|di|tions   com|pen|sa|tion   op|er|a|tions

Red words: would   could   another   walking

Challenge words: you ng   br ought   board   during   periods   calm   trouble   obey   recei ve   guilty   island   mouldy   tou gh   biscuit   sw ords   recruiting   qualifications   break   front   court   although   caught   washed

Vocabulary check: **superstitions** *beliefs that are not based on evidence*

irritable *easily annoyed*   **obey** *to follow a command*   **regulations** *rules made by someone in authority*

confiscation *taking away someone's property*   **marooning** *leaving someone trapped and alone*

infested *overrun, invaded*   **compensation** *something awarded to someone for their pain or suffering*

Grand theft at Bagshot Manor – an extended read

Vocabulary check: **suspect** *someone who might have committed a crime*

deny *to disagree with what someone has said*   **feeble** *weak and frail*

vicious *nasty and aggressive*

Survivors – an extended read

Vocabulary check: **bashful** *shy*   **anticipation** *expecting something*

pursed *make a rounded shape with your lips*   **raiding** *taking or stealing something*

ye *old English word meaning 'you' (plural)*   **thy** *old English word meaning 'your'*

thou *old English word meaning 'you' (singular)*   **mayst** *old English word meaning 'may'*

devious *underhand, shifty*   **remote** *distant, away from large numbers of people*